# HEROES
# GUIDE

Written by Jacqueline Rayner

**THE ADVENTURES OF MERLIN – THE HEROES GUIDE**

A BANTAM BOOK  978 0 553 82230 4

First published in Great Britain by Bantam,
an imprint of Random House Children's Books
A Random House Group Company

This edition published 2010

1 3 5 7 9 10 8 6 4 2

Text copyright © Bantam, 2010

© 2010 Shine Limited. Licensed by FremantleMedia Enterprises
Merlin created by Julian Jones, Jake Michie, Julian Murphy and Johnny Capps.

Bantam Books are published by Random House Children's Books,
61–63 Uxbridge Road, London W5 5SA

www.**rbooks**.co.uk
www.**kids**at**randomhouse**.co.uk

Addresses for companies within The Random House Group Limited can be found at:
www.**randomhouse**.co.uk/offices.htm

THE RANDOM HOUSE GROUP Limited Reg. No. 954009

A CIP catalogue record for this book is available from the British Library

Printed in China

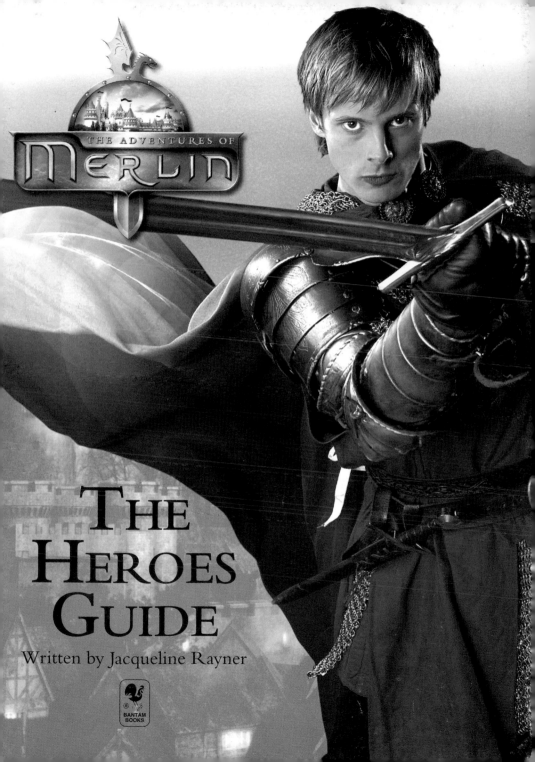

# THE ADVENTURES OF MERLIN

# THE HEROES GUIDE

Written by Jacqueline Rayner

BANTAM BOOKS

# CONTENTS

# WHAT IS A HERO?

**HERO (male); HEROINE (female);** Someone of distinguished courage or ability, admired for their brave deeds and noble qualities. They may have superhuman qualities which they use for good, sometimes to the disadvantage of themselves.

# FACE TO FACE

Can you count how many times each of our heroes' faces appear below?

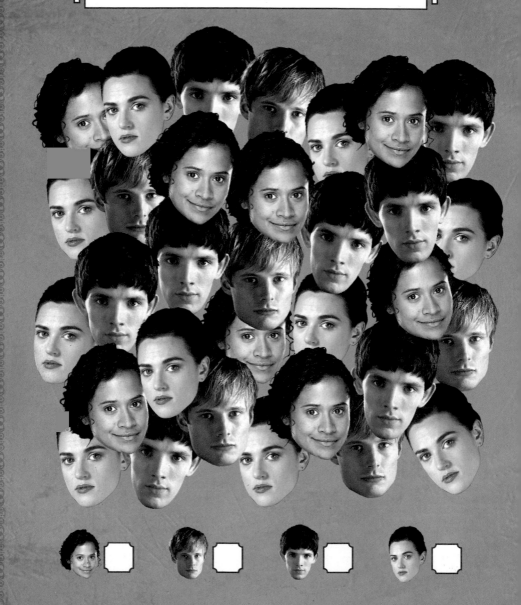

# HIDDEN HEROES

How many times is the word HERO
hidden in the wordsearch below?

```
H E R O Q Q I K B B D F G E K I H F D O
O P K O E H J I K B D F W O R E H Y F R
L Q F H E R O X B C J S D N K W F L P E
O G N K D D R S V H V H R B S W G S D H
Z D B T N F E M L Y E E H L U F N M B Y
H B V N K J H D S C C R E X B L O U T F
B E N K F B M L F B N M O M V O R E H B
G Q R D V B N M K L G D R V B C V E Y V
B B L O Q D G J L N F S E F V B M M V B
M V N O R E H E C V B N H E R O S C U C
L D F V G B N M K L O P Q A S X C V B H
U C V G T F H J K O X C V B M Q Z T E X
F C V Y W A Z L P R C V B N M W A R P X
H E R O X E N K P E Q P V Y O L O X A U
X Q V B N M K L O H Q Z V P U H F D T H
H C V B N M K Q Z P O R E H E G O P A F
U Q Z B N M K Y T F R X C V P L K T G O
O C O R E H H U R O E C V B N U M K L R
W W D C V B Y T R E H S A X B N M J U E
S F H I T O Y T D S V W A Z X C O R E H
```

**HERO** is hidden _____ times

# MERLIN

## MORE THAN A MANSERVANT

Those who know Merlin merely as Prince Arthur's manservant might laugh to hear him described as a hero, but that's undoubtedly what this young warlock is.

| HERO RATING | |
|---|---|
| Bravery | ★★★★★ |
| Magical power | ★★★★★ |
| Weapon prowess | ★★ |
| Selflessness | ★★★★★ |

## HERO IN DANGER

Merlin is gifted with great powers but they bring with them great danger. Although Merlin has battled against deadly magical monsters and the most powerful sorcerers in the land, the greatest threat to his safety is one that he must deal with every single day – the threat of discovery. If Uther ever finds out that Merlin is a sorcerer, he will have the boy executed. However, despite the risks, Merlin does not hesitate to use magic when others are in danger. Sometimes the consequences of his magic are not what he had planned, but he always acts with the best intentions.

# HEROIC DEEDS

Within days of arriving at Camelot, Merlin had saved Arthur from a would-be assassin, and his reward was to be made the prince's servant. Life at court has not been easy. When the sorceress Nimueh poisoned Arthur's cup, Merlin was ordered to drink from it. He did so knowing it might mean his death, but was prepared to sacrifice himself to save Arthur. As Merlin's destiny foretells, he continually puts himself in the way of danger in order to save his friend, the future king of Camelot.

## INDISCRIMINATE HERO

Merlin has acted indiscriminately to save both friends and enemies. Despite the terrible things that King Uther has done, Merlin has acted heroically to save his life on more than one occasion; often risking his own life in the process. He did so for Arthur's sake, and for the good of the kingdom, despite knowing that his own existence would be far easier if Uther had been left to perish and the ban on magic lifted.

## FEARLESS COURAGE

Perhaps Merlin's most heroic moment was his unarmed challenge to the Great Dragon. Hours after the death of his Dragonlord father, Merlin faced the beast despite not knowing whether he had inherited his father's ability to talk in Dragon-tongue. Regardless, he nobly confronted and defeated the beast. And rather than killing the Dragon, he showed great mercy by setting Kilgharrah free.

# A Modest Man

Merlin gets little, if any, recognition for his brave deeds. While he finds this difficult at times, he has never strayed from the path that was chosen for him. He has been offered power beyond compare, but he has always turned it down. Despite his heroics, the greatest warlock in the world remains ever humble.

# Heroic Words

'If it comes to a choice between saving people's lives and revealing who I really am – there is no choice.'

Merlin (*The Moment of Truth*)

'I willingly give my life for Arthur's.'

Merlin (*Le Morte D'Arthur*)

'Better to serve a good man than to rule with an evil one.'

Merlin (*The Curse of Cornelius Sigan*)

## Did You Know?

Merlin has learned that he is a Dragonlord, a very special warlock who can control Dragons.

# ARTHUR

| HERO RATING | |
|---|---|
| Bravery | ★★★★★ |
| Magical power | |
| Weapon prowess | ★★★★★ |
| Selflessness | ★★★★★ |

16

# HERO OR BULLY?

It's hard to imagine a more heroic figure than Prince Arthur! But while he's a fearless fighter, his other good qualities haven't always been so obvious. Gwen and Merlin both originally believed the prince to be a big-headed bully, and Arthur's reluctance to disobey his father has seen him carry out some very unpleasant tasks.

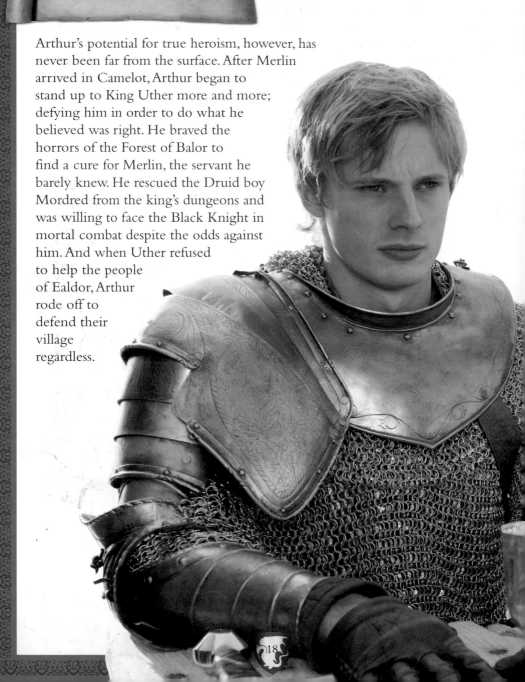

# HEROIC DEEDS

Arthur's potential for true heroism, however, has never been far from the surface. After Merlin arrived in Camelot, Arthur began to stand up to King Uther more and more; defying him in order to do what he believed was right. He braved the horrors of the Forest of Balor to find a cure for Merlin, the servant he barely knew. He rescued the Druid boy Mordred from the king's dungeons and was willing to face the Black Knight in mortal combat despite the odds against him. And when Uther refused to help the people of Ealdor, Arthur rode off to defend their village regardless.

# TRUE TEST OF CHARACTER

Arthur truly proved his character when he was tested at the Labyrinth of Gedref. He knew his pride had condemned his people to starve, and he was prepared to do anything to undo the damage. He drank what he believed was poison in order to rescue his people and save Merlin from death – mirroring the sacrifice Merlin once made for him. When the troll posing as Lady Catrina threatened Camelot, Arthur had little hesitation in once again drinking poison to free his father and the kingdom from her clutches.

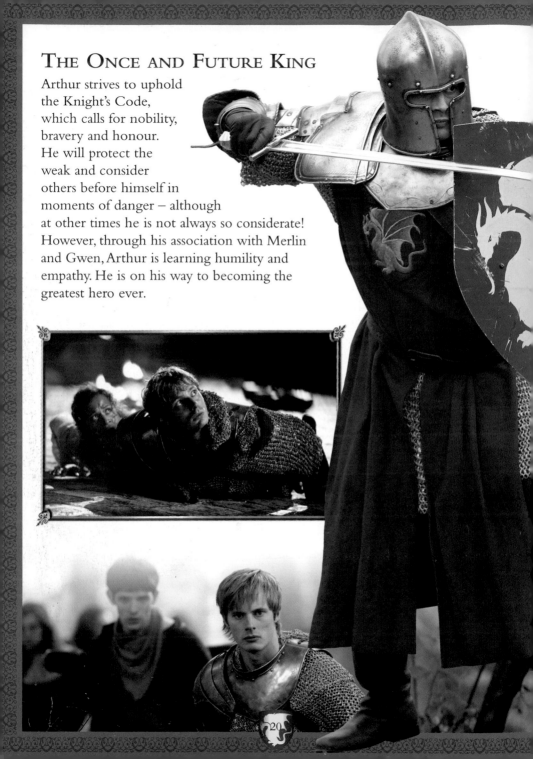

# THE ONCE AND FUTURE KING

Arthur strives to uphold
the Knight's Code,
which calls for nobility,
bravery and honour.
He will protect the
weak and consider
others before himself in
moments of danger – although
at other times he is not always so considerate!
However, through his association with Merlin
and Gwen, Arthur is learning humility and
empathy. He is on his way to becoming the
greatest hero ever.

# HEROIC WORDS

'I do not know what kind of king I will be. But I do have a sense of the kind of Camelot I would wish to live in. It would be where the punishment fits the crime.'

Arthur (*The Mark of Nimueh*)

'I brought this curse upon Camelot. I will lift it, or die trying.'

Arthur (*The Labyrinth of Gedref*)

'Arthur was willing to sacrifice his life to save yours. He has proven what is truly in his heart.'

Anhora to Merlin (*The Labyrinth of Gedref*)

'You are going to live to be the man I've seen inside you, Arthur. I can see a Camelot that is fair and just. I can see a king that the people will love and be proud to call their sovereign. For the love of Camelot, you have to live.'

Gwen to Arthur (*Le Morte D'Arthur*)

## DID YOU KNOW?

It is prophesied that Arthur is the once and future king who will unite the land of Albion.

# LIKE FATHER, LIKE SON

What are Merlin and his father thinking about?
Cross out all the letters that appear twice
to uncover their hidden thoughts.

X F F Y S
R A B K C N
S V O Y
X P Z K D G Z
P B V
C

**Answer:** __ __ __ __ __ __

# FOLLOW THE WORD

Merlin finds himself at the foot of a mountain which he must scale.
Help him to safety by following the word **CLIMB**
as it appears in the stones below.

| M | B | C | L | I | S | **FINISH** ↑ |
|---|---|---|---|---|---|---|
| Y | I | W | D | O | M | B |
| C | L | P | U | R | B | Z |
| B | I | L | C | M | S | |
| M | S | W | X | I | | |
| O | N | B | C | L | | |
| P | D | G | M | U | | |
| A | D | I | | | | |

**START** ➤ C    L

# WHAT WEAPON?
All knights must learn to fight with a variety of weapons. Can you name the weapons shown in the images below?

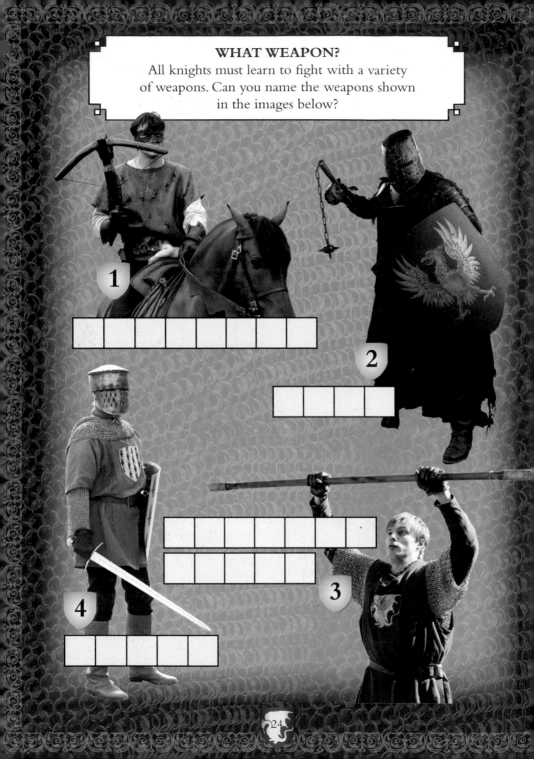

# SHIELD SPOTTING

Arthur's shield sports the golden dragon crest of Camelot. How many can you spot in the picture below? Look carefully: some of these shields are slightly different – Camelot's dragon is always gold and faces to the West.

**Answer:** ☐

# GWEN

## A SELFLESS SERVANT

Gwen's quiet, demure appearance hides a bold and heroic heart. Her thoughts are always for others before herself.

| HERO RATING | |
|---|---|
| Bravery | ★★★★ |
| Magical power | |
| Weapon prowess | ★★ |
| Selflessness | ★★★★★ |

# HEROIC DEEDS

Gwen braved the dungeons to obtain a
remedy for Merlin when he was poisoned
by Nimueh. She risked her job to take food
from the castle kitchens for starving villagers
during Anhora's curse. She stood up to
Prince Arthur when she insisted on fighting
to protect Merlin's home village of Ealdor,
and she helped Morgana flee from bandits
– allowing her mistress to escape at her own
expense.

# THE ONCE AND FUTURE QUEEN

But it is Gwen's quieter actions that have had the greatest effect on the kingdom. She teaches Arthur humility and thoughtfulness; she has challenged him when no one else would dare, and he has changed for the better through his love for her. It is clear that one day Arthur will be a better ruler because of Gwen.

## CHANGED FOR GOOD

It's not just Arthur that Gwen has influenced. She persuaded Gaius to save Uther from Edwin Muirden. Her love and faith reminded Lancelot of the noble aims once important to him. Even when Gwen was grieving for her father, she refused to give in to anger; insisting that revenge against Uther wouldn't help anyone. Many people have been changed for the better through their contact with this kind, courageous and selfless servant girl.

# HEROIC WORDS

'I've got to go. Merlin will die if I don't.'

Gwen (*The Poisoned Chalice*)

'Men aren't the only ones who can fight.'

Gwen (*The Moment of Truth*)

'Gwen gave herself up so that I might escape. I owe her my life.'

Morgana (*Lancelot and Guinevere*)

## DID YOU KNOW?

Gwen promised to love Lancelot for as long as she lives.

# GWEN'S GOOD DEEDS

Gwen is renowned for her good heart and quiet bravery.
Can you complete the grid by answering all the brave deeds
that Gwen has done.

## ACROSS

1. When the _ _ _ _ _ _ _ _ _ _ _
tries to make Morgana confess to
witchcraft, Gwen daringly helps
Merlin prove that Aredian is corrupt.
(11)

4. When gargoyles attack the city,
Gwen saves _ _ _ _ _ _ 's life. (6)

5. Uther sentences Gwen to
_ _ _ _ _ _ _ _ _ when he believes
she is guilty of witchcraft. (9)

## DOWN

2. Gwen is taken prisoner by the bandit
king _ _ _ _ _ _ _ .(7)

3. Gwen enters into battle against the
evil bandit _ _ _ _ _ who lays siege
to Merlin's home village. (5)

6. When King _ _ _ _ _ kills her father,
Gwen doesn't seek revenge. She
knows that to murder him would be
futile. It would make her no better
a person than the heartless king. (5)

# MORGANA

## HERO RATING

| | |
|---|---|
| Bravery | ★★★★★ |
| Magical power | ★★★ |
| Weapon prowess | ★★★ |
| Selflessness | ★★★ |

## A FORTHRIGHT WOMAN

The king's brave, veracious ward
has always been willing to stand up
for what she believes is right. No
consideration of her position in the
royal family or her personal safety has
ever stopped Morgana from following
her principles – no matter what the
consequences of her actions may be.

# Heroic Deeds

When Merlin brought a fugitive Druid boy to her chambers, she agreed to harbour him despite the danger to herself. She wielded a sword to help Merlin defend his home village against raiders, and hatched a daring escape plan to free herself and Gwen from kidnappers. Morgana has acted as Arthur's conscience on a number of occasions, urging him to do the right thing even though it meant opposing his father. Knowing this side of Morgana, it was hard for Merlin to believe the Great Dragon when he insisted she would one day form an evil pact with Mordred and bring about Arthur's doom.

## Bad Choices

Morgana's conflicts with Uther have often led her down a dark path. When Gwen's father was unfairly killed upon Uther's orders, Morgana plotted the king's murder with the sorcerer Tauren. Later, however, Morgana saw the humanity in Uther and had a change of heart, killing Tauren instead.

## Growing Powers

As Morgana became aware of her own magic, her resentment of Uther grew. So too did her sense of isolation and unease. Cut off from the Druids who offered her asylum, Morgana lived with the knowledge that if her guardian ever discovered that she had magic, he would have her imprisoned and killed like so many before her.

This made Morgana the perfect prey for the warlock Alvarr, who persuaded her to steal the powerful Crystal of Neahtid. At first Morgana refused, but Alvarr preyed on her weak spot. He made her feel part of an uprising of magical people fighting the king. Alvarr's plan failed and Uther sentenced him to death, which only strengthened Morgana's hatred of her guardian and she helped Alvarr escape. When Morgause returned to Camelot and asked Morgana whose side she was on, the answer was clear – any side that opposes Uther.

## Misplaced Honour

Although Morgana always believed she was fighting a just cause, she repeatedly aligned herself with callous and violent people, setting herself not only against Uther, but against Merlin, Arthur, and the rest of her kingdom too.

## A Fate Unknown

Morgana's life hangs in the balance. Taken from Camelot by her half-sister Morgause, does she know it was Merlin who poisoned her? And if she lives, will she return to Camelot a hero, or with villainy in her heart? Will she live up to the title of 'witch' bestowed on her by the Great Dragon? Only time will tell.

## Heroic Words

'I don't have a choice. I couldn't live with myself knowing I'd let Arthur die.'

> Morgana (*The Gates of Avalon*)

'I can't see an innocent child executed.'

> Morgana (*The Beginning of the End*)

'I have warned you about her in the past, but you have failed to take heed – she is dangerous. Although she doesn't know it, she has great power . . . And now she has chosen to turn her back on her own . . .'

> The Great Dragon to Merlin (*The Fires of Idirsholas*)

## Did You Know?

Morgana's father, Gorlois, was killed fighting for Uther.

# PICTURE PERFECT
Can you find the six pieces that will complete this
picture of the lovely Morgana?

# MORGANA'S MAZE

Morgana has become lost in the forest. Can you help her through
the maze to find the Druids that she seeks?

**START**

**FINISH**

# Gaius

| HERO RATING | |
|---|---|
| Bravery | ★★★★ |
| Magical power | ★★★ |
| Weapon prowess | ★ |
| Selflessness | ★★★★ |

## MENTOR AND PROTECTOR

Elderly court physician Gaius is not a typical hero. Though gifted with magic, he gave up sorcery long ago. When magic was banned by Uther, Gaius officially recanted his loyalty to the old religion and has since been blamed by other magic-users for standing by and doing nothing during the Great Purge. For many years he has been a loyal servant to Uther, often serving his king rather than his conscience. But when his old friend Hunith appealed to him to look after her only son, Merlin, his life took a different path. Gaius soon found himself having to make very difficult choices.

# Heroic Deeds

Gaius' decision to protect and guide Merlin is perhaps even more heroic because hiding the boy's gift from Uther is not easy for him. But despite his scruples, Gaius has protected Merlin's secret, defied the king and used magic himself, risking his own life to save others.

## The Ultimate Sacrifice

When Gaius saw that Merlin was determined to give up his own life to Nimueh, he made the ultimate sacrifice – he died in Merlin's place. Merlin's mastery of life and death ultimately revived Gaius, but this was not the last time the physician showed how much he would give up for the boy. In order to protect Merlin and Morgana from Aredian, the witchfinder, Gaius confessed to sorcery. He was sentenced to death, and was only saved at the last moment. Mentoring Merlin is a dangerous task – but Gaius has risen to the challenge admirably.

# HEROIC WORDS

'I will not allow you to kill Uther.'

Gaius to Edwin (*A Remedy to Cure All Ills*)

'To have known you has been my greatest pleasure and to sacrifice myself for you is but an honour.'

Gaius' letter to Merlin (*Le Morte D'Arthur*)

'With all my powers of prediction, I could never have foretold this — Gaius the hero.'

Nimueh (*Le Morte D'Arthur*)

'Gaius has served me with unfailing dedication. Without his wisdom and his knowledge I would not be sitting here today.'

Uther (*The Witchfinder*)

## DID YOU KNOW?

Gaius was made a freeman of Camelot for saving Uther's life.

# LANCELOT

## AN HONOURABLE FIGHTER

When Lancelot was a child, his village was attacked by raiders from the Northern Plains. Lancelot was the only survivor. From that day on he has been determined to fight evil, and he devoted his life to training in the art of combat.

| HERO RATING | |
|---|---|
| Bravery | ★★★★★ |
| Magical power | |
| Weapon prowess | ★★★★★ |
| Selflessness | ★★★★★ |

# Heroic Deeds

Merlin first encountered Lancelot when the young man saved him from a fearsome Griffin. Lancelot's ambition was to become a knight of Camelot, but only those of noble birth could qualify. Merlin lied to Arthur to give Lancelot a chance to try out for a knighthood but Lancelot was reluctant to go along with the deception.

When the truth was discovered, Lancelot was arrested but Arthur released him. Lancelot refused to leave while the prince might be in danger, so he followed Arthur into battle and, with Merlin's help, bravely fought and killed the Griffin.

## Falling in Love

Lancelot saw Merlin use magic and, while he vowed to keep the boy's secret, he refused to take credit for defeating the Griffin alone. Ashamed of his earlier dishonesty, Lancelot left Camelot. This was a particularly difficult sacrifice as Lancelot had fallen in love with Gwen.

## BRIEF ENCOUNTERS

Lancelot had to give up his dream of becoming a knight and instead earn his living fighting for money. He was fighting for Hengist when he saw Gwen, who had been kidnapped. Lancelot bravely risked his life to rescue Gwen, but was captured while buying her time to escape.

When Lancelot and Gwen were eventually freed – rescued by Arthur and Merlin – Lancelot realized that the crown prince was also deeply in love with Gwen. Lancelot's noble nature and loyalty to Arthur would not allow him to stand between them and he once more left Gwen's side – heroically and painfully sacrificing his own feelings to do what he believed was right.

## HEROIC WORDS

'Arthur stands in mortal peril. I must do what I can to protect him. It is my duty, knight or not.'

Lancelot (*Lancelot and Guinevere*)

'You have reminded me of who I am. I will die with faith in my heart. That is worth more than anything.'

Lancelot to Gwen (*Lancelot and Guinevere*)

## DID YOU KNOW?

Lancelot posed as the fifth son of Lord Eldred of Northumbria – but King Uther knew that Eldred only had four sons.

## RIDDLE ME THIS

Gaius is a very smart man but he's struggling to find
the answers to these riddles. Can you help him?

1. What can run but never walks, has a mouth
but never talks, has a head but never weeps,
and has a hed but never sleeps?

\_ \_ \_ \_ \_

2. What is light as a feather, but even the strongest
man cannot hold it more than a few minutes?

\_ \_ \_ \_ \_ \_

3. Pronounced as one letter but written with three,
Only two different letters are used to make me;
I'm double, I'm single. I'm black, blue, and grey;
I'm read from both ends and the same either way.

\_ \_ \_

4. I pass before the sun, yet make no shadow.
What am I?

\_ \_ \_ \_

5. Mountains will crumble and temples
will fall, and no man can survive its
endless call. What is it?

\_ \_ \_ \_

BREATH    RIVER

TIME    WIND    EYE

46

A B C D E F G H I J K L M N O P Q R S T U V W X Y Z

## BREAK THE CODE

Using the rune guide on the left, can you decipher
what Lancelot has written?

___ ___ ____ _____ __

___ _____ _____

__ _____ __ ___

__ _____ __ ___

_____ _____ ____

_____ , _____

_____ , _____

____ _____ ____

_____ _____

_____ .

# HUNITH

| HERO RATING | |
|---|---|
| Bravery | ★★★★ |
| Magical power | |
| Weapon prowess | ★★ |
| Selflessness | ★★★★★ |

## A MOTHER'S LOVE

Hunith's heroism is the sort of quiet bravery displayed by many mothers – always doing what she believes is best for her child, despite the pain it might cause her. After caring for Merlin and protecting his secret, Hunith realized he was no longer safe in Ealdor. Though she would miss him terribly, Hunith sent her son to Camelot where Gaius could better protect and guide him.

# HEROIC DEEDS

Hunith is also capable of other sorts of bravery. When bandits besieged Ealdor, she stood up to them. She visited Camelot to beg for Uther's help, and then returned to Ealdor to fight when her pleas did not succeed. When Arthur came to Ealdor, Hunith bravely battled by his side to save her village.

## UNINTENDED VICTIM

Even when Hunith appears to be dying, an accidental victim of Merlin's bargain with Nimueh, her thoughts are not for herself but for her son. It is a testament to her goodness and kindness that Merlin is willing to give up his life for her. Thankfully, both mother and son are spared.

## HEROIC WORDS

'It is every mother's fate to think her child is special, and yet I would give my life that Merlin were not so.'

Hunith to Gaius (*The Dragon's Call*)

'I'll follow you. If I'm to die, then I want to go out fighting.'

Hunith to Arthur (*The Moment of Truth*)

### DID YOU KNOW?

Hunith is an old friend of Gaius', and knows that he was once a sorcerer.

# WILLIAM OF EALDOR

| HERO RATING | |
|---|---|
| Bravery | ★★★ |
| Magical power | |
| Weapon prowess | ★★★ |
| Selflessness | ★★★★ |

## A CHILDHOOD FRIEND

As Merlin's childhood friend, he was the only other person, apart from Hunith, who knew Merlin's secret. When Merlin returned home to find Ealdor besieged by the bandit, Kanan, Will believed Merlin should use his powers to protect his friends and family, and risk the consequences of his magical abilities being discovered.

# Heroic Deeds

Threatened by Merlin's new friendships, Will disliked Arthur on sight. He feared the prince's plans to fight Kanan would send them all to their graves. When the people of Ealdor chose to fight with Arthur, Will left. However, he couldn't abandon his people for long, and he returned just in time to save Merlin's life.

## Saving the Day

When Merlin used his powers to save the day, Arthur realized there must be a sorcerer in Ealdor. But before the prince could investigate, Kanan fired a crossbow at him. Despite his dislike of Arthur, Will didn't hesitate – he pushed the prince out of the way and took the crossbow bolt himself. Dying, Will made one last heroic gesture. He told Arthur that *he* was the sorcerer so that Merlin's secret would not be exposed.

## Heroic Words

'You're a good man, Merlin, a great man. And one day you're going to be servant to a great king. Now you can still make that happen.'

Will (*The Moment of Truth*)

## Did You Know?

Will hated the nobility because his father was killed fighting for King Cenred.

## HURRY HOME

When Merlin heard that his home town was under siege from dangerous bandits, he rushed back to help his friends and family. Can you guide him home?

Camelot

Ealdor

## FIND A FRIEND

Will was a real hero and true friend to Merlin.
How many words can you make from the letters in the word
FRIENDSHIP?

friend    fire

# BROTHERS IN ARMS

Merlin, Arthur, Morgana and Gwen all joined together to help defeat the bandit Kanan. Look carefully at the pictures below. Can you spot the eight differences between them?

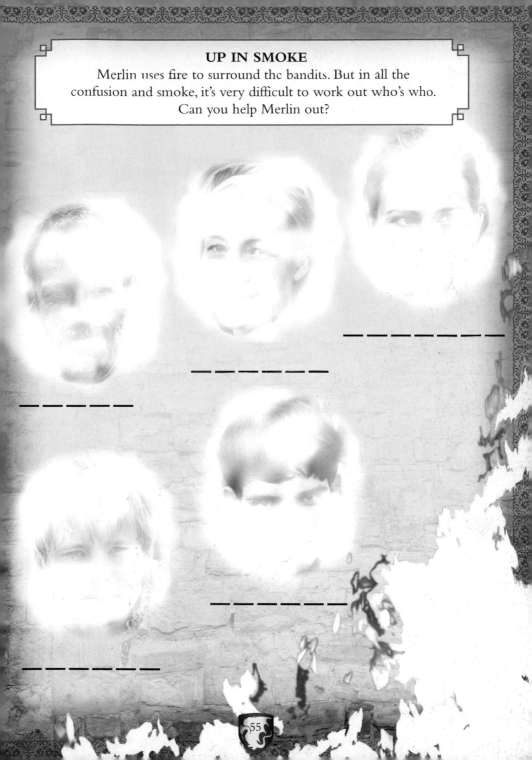

# UP IN SMOKE
Merlin uses fire to surround the bandits. But in all the
confusion and smoke, it's very difficult to work out who's who.
Can you help Merlin out?

_ _ _ _ _ _ _

_ _ _ _ _ _

_ _ _ _ _

_ _ _ _ _ _

_ _ _ _ _ _ _

# SIR BEDIVERE

| HERO RATING | |
|---|---|
| Bravery | ★★★★ |
| Magical power | |
| Weapon prowess | ★★★★ |
| Selflessness | ★★★★★ |

## A KNIGHT'S FATE

Sir Bedivere's heroism was all the more striking because it was not glorious. He did not die in a great battle, or while defending the realm. Instead, he met a gory and horrific end at the claws of the Questing Beast.

## HEROIC DEEDS

During a hunting trip, Prince Arthur's party was attacked by a beast with the body of a leopard and the head of a snake. Merlin fell, and would have died if Arthur and Sir Bedivere hadn't saved him. But in helping Merlin, Bedivere found himself at the mercy of the terrible monster.

Bedivere showed no hesitation in running into danger to save someone who, as far as he knew, was just a servant boy. He paid a terrible price for his heroism.

# HEROIC WORDS

*'Where's Sir Bedivere?'*  Merlin (*Le Morte D'Arthur*)

## DID YOU KNOW?

The Knight's Code states that all knights should act with honour and gallantry, protect the innocent and display courtly manners.

# Sir Pelinor and Sir Owain

## Noble Knights of Camelot

Camelot was placed in great peril when the sorceress Nimueh conjured a wraith, in the form of the Black Knight, to take revenge on King Uther. He threw down the gauntlet in front of the king and Arthur – a challenge to single combat. Arthur went to pick it up but Sir Owain took it first, eager to prove himself and face an enemy on behalf of his king. Even when the Black Knight announced that the fight would be to the death, Owain showed no fear.

## Heroic Deeds

Owain bravely and confidently went into the arena. He dealt a deadly blow to the Black Knight, but the wraith could not be killed by a mortal weapon. The undead knight did not fall, but instead killed Owain.

| HERO RATING | |
|---|---|
| Bravery | ★★★ |
| Magical power | |
| Weapon prowess | ★★★★ |
| Selflessness | ★★★ |

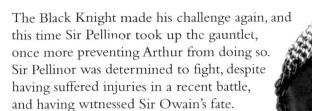

The Black Knight made his challenge again, and this time Sir Pellinor took up the gauntlet, once more preventing Arthur from doing so. Sir Pellinor was determined to fight, despite having suffered injuries in a recent battle, and having witnessed Sir Owain's fate.

During combat, Pellinor knocked the Black Knight's sword from his hand. He followed this up with what should have been a mortal blow. But, as in the earlier fight, the Black Knight did not fall. He went on to kill Pellinor. The magic of the wraith robbed Camelot of two of its bravest defenders.

# HEROIC WORDS

'*I know no one braver.*'

Arthur to Sir Owain (*Excalibur*)

'*Sir Pellinor is more than a match for him.*'

Uther (*Excalibur*)

## DID YOU KNOW?

Morgana sent Sir Owain a red ribbon to wear for luck.

# KEEP A LOOK OUT
Take a careful look at the pictures of knights in training.
Can you spot the eight differences between them?

## WHAT'S IN A NAME?

Can you fill in the missing letters that will complete the words on the left and right and reveal the missing word?

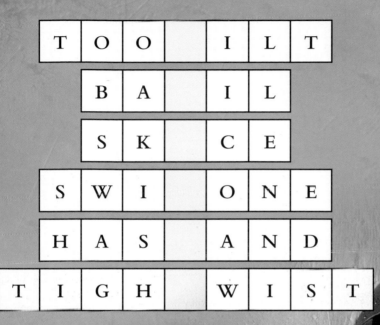

| T | O | O | | I | L | T |
|---|---|---|---|---|---|---|

| | B | A | | I | L | |
|---|---|---|---|---|---|---|

| | S | K | | C | E | |
|---|---|---|---|---|---|---|

| S | W | I | | O | N | E |
|---|---|---|---|---|---|---|

| H | A | S | | A | N | D |
|---|---|---|---|---|---|---|

| T | I | G | H | | W | I | S | T |
|---|---|---|---|---|---|---|---|---|

**The answer is:**

# SIR GERAINT

| HERO RATING | |
|---|---|
| Bravery | ★★★ |
| Magical power | |
| Weapon prowess | ★★★ |
| Selflessness | ★★ |

# A Call to Arms

When the deadly gargoyles – brought to life by Cornelius Sigan –
attacked Camelot, Uther ordered the citadel to be sealed so the monsters
couldn't get in. But Arthur defied his father and left the palace, knowing
there were people trapped on the drawbridge. Sir Geraint was one of the
brave knights who followed Arthur, although tragically their mission was
unsuccessful – the people had been slaughtered by the time they arrived.

# Heroic Deeds

A winged gargoyle attacked the
knights, and Sir Geraint fought at
Arthur's side. Eventually they were
driven back towards the castle. Set
upon by one of Sigan's monsters,
Arthur ordered his knights to save
themselves. Assuming control of the
squad, Sir Geraint's top priority was
the safety of his men, so he reluctantly
ordered them to retreat – and shut the
door on the prince.

## Serving the King

When Uther realized Arthur was
missing, he tried to leave the palace to
look for his son. Sir Geraint restrained
him, warning that opening the doors
would mean death for them all.
Although Geraint did
not wish to leave Arthur
to the mercy of the
gargoyles, his duty was
to protect the king and
those who had found
sanctuary in the castle.
But however much Sir
Geraint believed he was
doing the right thing,
challenging King Uther
was a very brave act
indeed . . .

# HEROIC WORDS

'Retreat, retreat! Seal the doors!'

Sir Geraint (*The Curse of Cornelius Sigan*)

'You can't go out there, sire! If you open that door, you will die . . . We will all die.'

Sir Geraint (*The Curse of Cornelius Sigan*)

## DID YOU KNOW?

Sir Geraint fights left-handed – an advantage against many opponents.

# FILL IN THE BLANKS

Can you help complete this grid?
Every column and box must contain each of the six faces below.

# TAKING AIM

Can you help Arthur with his target practice? Follow the right path to help his arrow hit the shield.

A

B

C

1

2

3

ANSWER

# AGLAIN

| HERO RATING | |
|---|---|
| Bravery | ★★★ |
| Magical power | ★★★ |
| Weapon prowess | ★★ |
| Selflessness | ★★★★ |

## AN OFFER OF SANCTURY

Uther believes that all Druids are evil but Aglain's selfless actions proved that the king is wrong. When Morgana feared she had magic, she fled to the Forest of Ascetir to seek answers from the Druids. Alone and lost in the woods, she was attacked by serkets – huge scorpion-like creatures – and would have perished had Aglain not come to her rescue.

# HEROIC DEEDS

Aglain brought Morgana to the Druid camp. He assured her that magic was a gift, and promised her a safe home. Just as Morgana began to contemplate a life with the Druids, Arthur and his knights arrived to 'rescue' her. Still in pain from the serket wound, Morgana could not flee, so Aglain bravely stayed by her side. Moments later, he was tragically shot by Arthur's men.

# HEROIC WORDS

'In time you will learn that magic isn't a dark art that must be shrouded in secrecy. It can be a force for good.'

Aglain to Morgana (*The Nightmare Begins*)

'We're not leaving you behind.'

Aglain to Morgana (*The Nightmare Begins*)

## DID YOU KNOW?

Like many Druids, Aglain was able to communicate with his mind.

# FREYA

| HERO RATING | |
|---|---|
| Bravery | ★★★★ |
| Magical power | ★★★ |
| Weapon prowess | |
| Selflessness | ★★★ |

## BEAUTY OR THE BEAST?

When Merlin discovered Freya chained in a cage in the street, the victim of one of Uther's bounty hunters, he knew that the sad, haunted-looking Druid girl must have magic. Merlin helped her escape and risked everything to keep her hidden from Uther. He brought her food and tried to cheer her up, and a powerful bond quickly formed between the pair. But despite her affection for Merlin, Freya warned him to stay away from her; insisting she wasn't worthy of his kindness.

# Heroic Deeds

Merlin couldn't stay away from Freya. Even when it became obvious that Freya was no longer safe in Camelot, a besotted Merlin decided he would give up his destiny to move away with her.

## A Dark Secret

But there was much Merlin didn't know about his new friend. When Freya first arrived in Camelot, people started falling victim to a deadly creature – a huge black cat with wings. Gaius suspected that Freya was really a Bastet; a human who turned into a monster in the night, against their will.

Gaius was right: Freya was indeed a Bastet, and her story was a tragic one. Years earlier, Freya accidently killed a man in self-defence. To punish her, the man's mother – a sorceress – cursed her to go on killing for the rest of her life so she could never again be close to another human. Freya tried to stay away from people so she couldn't do any harm but every morning she woke as a girl, burdened with the terrible knowledge that she had taken innocent lives during the night. Her life was a disturbed and lonely one – until she met Merlin.

## The Final Release

Fatally wounded by Arthur while in beast form, Freya knew she would soon finally be free of her curse. But she would not die alone, or lonely; Freya passed away in Merlin's arms, thankful that someone at last knew her as a girl and not a monster. And, what's more, he loved her.

# Heroic Words

'The ancient chronicles speak of a heinous curse. It dooms its victim to turn each night, at the stroke of midnight, into a vicious and bloodthirsty beast.'

Gaius (*The Lady of the Lake*)

'Whatever she is and whatever she's done, she doesn't deserve to die.'

Merlin (*The Lady of the Lake*)

'You've already saved me. You made me feel loved.'

Freya to Merlin (*The Lady of the Lake*)

## Did You Know?

Merlin laid Freya to rest in the same lake where he once threw Excalibur.

# BALINOR

## LAST OF HIS KIND

When the Great Dragon attacked Camelot, Merlin learned that only those known as Dragonlords can control dragons. One such man had survived the Great Purge – Balinor. It was he who captured the Great Dragon for Uther, only agreeing to because he believed the king wanted to make peace, not imprison the beast. Uther then turned on the Dragonlords themselves; hunting them down like animals because he feared their magic.

## AN ABSENT FATHER

Gaius helped Balinor escape to Ealdor, where he stayed with Hunith. They fell in love, but soon even Ealdor was no longer safe – Balinor had to leave. For years he lived as a hermit in the forests and caves of Cenred's kingdom, unaware that the woman he still loved had borne him a son – Merlin.

| HERO RATING | |
|---|---|
| Bravery | ★★★★ |
| Magical power | ★★★★★ |
| Weapon prowess | ★★★★ |
| Selflessness | ★★★★★ |

# HEROIC DEEDS

When Balinor first learned of Camelot's plight, he refused to help because of his hatred of Uther. But he finally agreed when Merlin reminded him of Gaius, and the kindness the brave physician once showed him.

On their way back to Camelot, just as father and son began to bond, Cenred's men attacked their camp. Balinor bravely saved his son, but was run through with a sword and killed.

## A NEW POWER

Merlin was devastated, but when he next faced the Great Dragon he felt a new power surge within him. Merlin heard his father's voice in his mind, and felt his presence. Balinor might be dead, but to his son – the last Dragonlord – he will never be far away.

## HEROIC WORDS

'I understand how Kilgharrah feels. He's lost every one of his kind, every one of his kin.'

Balinor to Merlin (*The Last Dragonlord*)

'You don't choose to become a Dragonlord . . . It is not something you're taught. It is a sacred gift. For thousands of years it has been handed down from father to son. And that is what you, Merlin, must become.'

Balinor (*The Last Dragonlord*)

'Like all Dragonlords you won't know for sure that you have that power until you face your first Dragon.'

Balinor to Merlin (*The Last Dragonlord*)

## DID YOU KNOW?

When a Dragonlord commands a Dragon he cannot speak in any human language – he must find a voice deep inside himself that only he and the Dragons share.

# DRAGONLORD DREAMING

In Merlin's dream he's trying to reach his father. Can you guide him through the maze to Balinor?

**FINISH**

**START**

# DRAW A DRAGON

Using the picture on the grid below, can you create
your very own Dragon in the larger grid underneath it?
Use your pens and pencils to colour it in!

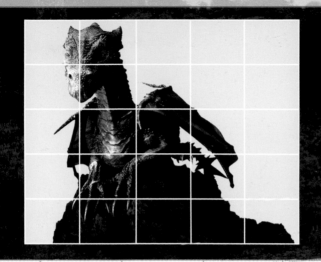

# SIR WILLIAM OF DEIRA

| HERO RATING | |
|---|---|
| Bravery | ★★ |
| Magical power | |
| Weapon prowess | |
| Selflessness | ★ |

## THE FARMER KNIGHT

Prince Arthur decided to enter a jousting tournament in disguise to prove that he could win a competition on skill alone – and not just because of his title as Crown Prince of Camelot. He needed someone to act as his 'public face' in the tournament, and Merlin selected William.

# HEROIC DEEDS

William was used to a humble existence as a farmer in one of Camelot's outlying villages. Then he suddenly found himself in the big city; bathed, groomed, and dressed in noble's clothes. And then he had to pretend to be a knight!

Riding out onto the tournament ground in front of King Uther and the knights and nobles of Camelot would be pretty daunting for anyone. For William, who had never sat on a powerful jousting horse before, it was an act of extreme bravery! After successfully masquerading as 'Sir William of Deira' for the entire tournament, William definitely deserved the adulation he got from the crowd.

# HEROIC WORDS

'Imagine you're really arrogant. Knights like to think they're so much better than everyone else.'

Merlin to William (*The Once and Future Queen*)

'Polish my armour, boy.'

William to Merlin (*The Once and Future Queen*)

'The ladies of the court are quite impressed with Sir William. They think he's very handsome.'

Gwen (*The Once and Future Queen*)

## DID YOU KNOW?

William was not sure how to acknowledge the crowd – Arthur had to instruct him on how to wave.

# UTHER

## HERO RATING

| | |
|---|---|
| Bravery | ★★★ |
| Magical power | |
| Weapon prowess | ★★★★★ |
| Selflessness | ★★ |

## AN UNUSUAL HERO

Uther a hero? Not many people would agree. He has sanctioned the deaths of hundreds of people, many of whom were innocent.

## THE GREATER GOOD

It is important to remember that Uther genuinely thinks a war on magic is the best thing for his people. He believes magic is a destructive and corrupting force; by banning it he is trying to keep his kingdom peaceful and prosperous.

Uther might not be an out-and-out villain but his often violent and hard-hearted behaviour stems from guilt and fear, which don't make him seem very heroic. Uther's hatred of sorcery is caused by grief over the loss of his wife, Ygraine, and from an awareness that it was his own one-time involvement with magic that brought about her death.

# Heroic Deeds

In his role as a father, Uther's more heroic qualities come to the fore. When Gaius and Merlin needed him to cry tears of regret to break the troll queen's enchantment, they knew the only way to his heart was through Arthur. And, indeed, when Uther thought he had lost his son he was inconsolable. The king loves Arthur dearly, and has been prepared to give up his life for the boy. When Arthur challenged the Black Knight to a duel, Uther fought the wraith rather than risk his son's life.

Uther would do anything to protect Arthur – both because he loves his son, and because he believes that Camelot needs Arthur as its king in the future. The actions Uther has taken to keep Arthur safe have often alienated the prince, but he always believed he was acting for the best.

## Heroic Words

'You have always done what you believe to be right.'

Gaius to Uther (*A Remedy to Cure All Ills*)

'Ygraine gave up life for him, so must I.'

Uther (*Excalibur*)

'The fate of Camelot rests in my hands. It is my responsibility to protect the people of this land from its enemies.'

Uther (*To Kill the King*)

'Despite Uther's failings he has brought peace and prosperity to this kingdom.'

Gaius (*To Kill the King*)

## Did You Know?

Uther did not inherit the throne, but made himself king by conquering all opponents and bringing peace to the land.

# THE GREAT DRAGON

| HERO RATING | |
|---|---|
| Bravery | ★★★ |
| Magical power | ★★★★★ |
| Weapon prowess | |
| Selflessness | |

# A Mighty Beast

Those who witnessed the devastation inflicted on Camelot by the Great Dragon, Kilgharrah, would find it hard to think of it as a force for good. Yet without the Dragon's help, many more tragedies would have befallen the kingdom. Its advice enabled Merlin to save Arthur's life many times, but its wisdom was not reserved for keeping the prince safe. The Dragon told Merlin how to defeat the Afanc, a monster that was poisoning the city's water supply, and later gave Merlin a spell to conquer the ancient sorcerer Sigan, who tried to raze Camelot to the ground.

# Heroic Deeds

The Dragon's desire to see Arthur become king, grant it its freedom and allow magic to return to the kingdom was born out of selfishness. But it's hard to hold that against it. After all, this magnificent, mighty and ancient beast had been held captive underground for over twenty years!

## Blinded by Rage

When Merlin released it, the Great Dragon realized it could never truly feel free; thanks to Uther it was the last of its kind and magic had all but disappeared. The Dragon's anger and grief drove it to seek revenge.

Kilgharrah's rage did not subside until Merlin became a Dragonlord and overpowered it in the final battle. When Merlin chose to spare its life, the Great Dragon agreed to show the same mercy to others as the warlock had shown to it.

But just before it left Camelot, Kilgharrah declared that it and Merlin would one day cross paths again. It remains to be seen whether this was just a guess, or one of the Great Dragon's prophecies?

# HEROIC WORDS

'Free this land from tyranny, Merlin. Free us all!'

The Great Dragon (*To Kill the King*)

'You have it in your power to prevent a great evil.'

The Great Dragon to Merlin (*The Beginning of the End*)

'I am the last of my kind, Merlin. Whatever wrongs I have done, do not make me responsible for the death of my noble breed.'

The Great Dragon (*The Last Dragonlord*)

## DID YOU KNOW?

A Dragon's heart is on its right side, not its left.

# WHICH HERO ARE YOU?

Are you more magical than mighty? Do you have more beauty than brains?

Answer these questions to find out which hero you're most like!

## Q1

How would you rate your fighting skills?

a) Amazing! ○
b) Not bad ○
c) If someone was attacking a person I loved, then I'd do anything in a fight ○

## Q2

Someone is behaving unjustly, do you:

a) Draw your sword and challenge them to a duel ○
b) Quietly work some magic to spoil their plans ○
c) Let them know that they're acting badly and they should stop straight away ○

## Q3

What do you fear?

a) Nothing! ○
b) Letting people down ○
c) Harm coming to my friends and family ○

## Q4

How do you treat others?

a) I try to treat everyone as an equal but sometimes I find it hard ○
b) I'm nice to everyone who deserves it ○
c) I treat people the way I would like them to treat me ○

## Q5

You see a friend in danger, do you:

a) Jump in straight away
b) Wait for back-up
c) Scream for help

## Q7

What's your greatest weapon?

a) My sword
b) My tricks
c) My smile

## Q6

What are your thoughts on magic?

a) Sorcery is only for the weak and evil
b) It's great to get you out of a sticky spot
c) I don't think that magic is always used for evil

## Q8

What three words best describe you?

a) Strong, determined, quick-tempered
b) Quiet, modest, confident
c) Loyal, friendly, kind

## Mostly A's
### ARTHUR

You're as strong-willed as you are strong! Always prepared to put up a fight against injustice you're a brave hero but beware, sometimes you can act rashly without thinking about the consequences of your actions.

## Mostly B's
### MERLIN

A smart and quick-witted hero, you're more prepared to use your brains and mental powers rather than physical strength. People know they can rely on your good sense and fast thinking.

## Mostly C's
### GWEN

Loyal and kind-hearted you are a good friend who is never afraid to speak your mind and will always heroically stand up against any injustice you see.

# ANSWERS

8    6    8    10

Page 9

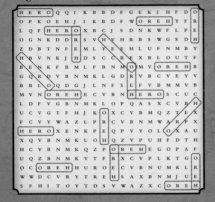

Page 22

DRAGON

Page 23

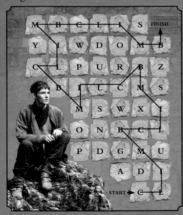

Page 24

1. CROSSBOW  2. MACE
3. QUARTERSTAFF
4. SWORD

Page 25

5

Page 31

1. WITCHFINDER  2. HENGIST
3. KANEN  4. ARTHUR  5. EXECUTION
6. UTHER

Page 36

SPACE 1 MATCHES JIGSAW PIECE A;
2=C,  3=D,  4=F,  5=G,  6=E

Page 37

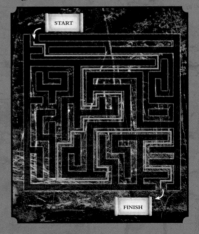

Page 46

1. RIVER  2. BREATH,  3. EYE,
4. WIND  5. TIME

Page 47

LANCELOT'S MESSAGE READS:

It is the duty of every noble knight of
Camelot to act with honour and gallantry,
protect the innocent and display courtly
manners.

Page 52

Page 53

Well done if you got any of the following words:
den, dens, die, dies, din, dine, diner, diners, dines,
dip, dips, dire, dish, dishier, dries, drip, drips, end,
ends, fed, fen, fend, fends, fens, fern, ferns, fie, fiend,
fiendish, fiends, find, finder, finds, fine, fined, finer,
finish, finished, fins, fir, fire, fired, fires, firs, fish, fished,
fishier, fresh, fried, friend, friends, friendship, fries, he,
heir, heirs, hen, hens, her, herd, herds, hers, hi, hid,
hide, hides, hind, hinder, hinders, hip, hips, hire, hired,
hires, his, ides, if, in, infer, infers, inside, insider, inspire,
inspired, ire, iris, is, nip, nips, pen, pens, per, perish, pie,
pied, pier, piers, pies, pin, pine, pined, pines, pins, pride,
pried, pries, prise, prised, red, reds, refinish, rein, reins,
rend, rends, resin, rid, ride, rides, rids, rife, rind, rinds,
rinse, rinsed, rip, ripe, ripen, ripens, rips, rise, risen,
send, serf, serif, she, shed, shied, shin, shine, shined,
shiner, shinier, ship, shire, shred, shrine, side, sip, sir,
sire, sired, siren, snide, snider, snip, snipe, sniped, sniper,
sped, spend, spider, spied, spin, spine, spinier, spire

Page 54

Page 55

Page 60

Page 61
KNIGHT

Page 66

Page 67

PATH C WILL TAKE ARTHUR'S ARROW
TO THE SHIELD.

Page 76

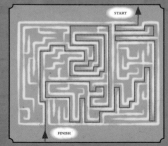

# THE ADVENTURES OF MERLIN:
## EPISODE GUIDE
### Series 1

**Episode 1 – *The Dragon's Call***
When Merlin arrived in Camelot he was full of excitement and eager for adventure. But sorcery is outlawed in Camelot and so began his struggle to keep his magical powers a closely guarded secret.

**Episode 2 – *Valiant***
When a mysterious knight appeared for the tournament, Merlin instantly suspected that dark magic was afoot. He was determined to investigate, but soon found that keeping his secret – and Prince Arthur alive – was harder than he thought . . .

**Episode 3 – *The Mark of Nimueh***
When a water-borne plague swept through Camelot, Merlin embarked on a dangerous search to uncover the source and the sorcerer responsible. Little did he know that this would not be his last encounter with the powerful sorceress Nimueh.

**Episode 4 – *The Poisoned Chalice***
After Merlin thwarted her first plan for revenge, Nimueh returned to Camelot with a plan to poison Arthur. Merlin unwittingly drank from the poisoned cup meant for the prince and as his servant lay dying, Arthur bravely set off on a quest to find the remedy.

**Episode 5 – *Lancelot***
A young man saved Merlin from a deadly Griffin attack. Eternally grateful Merlin took Lancelot back to the palace in the hope that he might make his saviour's dream come true – to become a knight of Camelot.

**Episode 6 – *A Remedy to Cure All Ills***
When Edwin Muirden arrived in Camelot to challenge Gaius' role as court physician Gaius was forced to choose between Uther's life and keeping Merlin's secret. And Merlin had to decide whether to use his magic for good or ill.

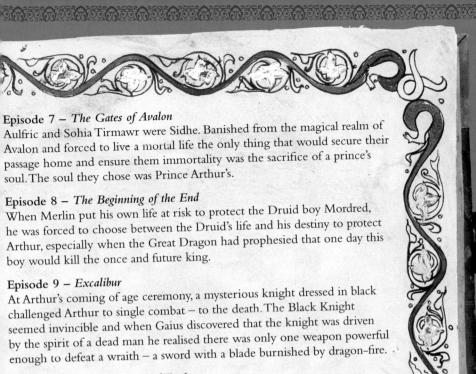

## Episode 7 – *The Gates of Avalon*

Aulfric and Sohia Tirmawr were Sidhe. Banished from the magical realm of Avalon and forced to live a mortal life the only thing that would secure their passage home and ensure them immortality was the sacrifice of a prince's soul. The soul they chose was Prince Arthur's.

## Episode 8 – *The Beginning of the End*

When Merlin put his own life at risk to protect the Druid boy Mordred, he was forced to choose between the Druid's life and his destiny to protect Arthur, especially when the Great Dragon had prophesied that one day this boy would kill the once and future king.

## Episode 9 – *Excalibur*

At Arthur's coming of age ceremony, a mysterious knight dressed in black challenged Arthur to single combat – to the death. The Black Knight seemed invincible and when Gaius discovered that the knight was driven by the spirit of a dead man he realised there was only one weapon powerful enough to defeat a wraith – a sword with a blade burnished by dragon-fire.

## Episode 10 – *The Moment of Truth*

When Merlin's home town was besieged by bandits and King Uther refused to send his knights to help, Merlin and his friends headed back to Ealdor to drive the outlaws away.

## Episode 11 – *The Labyrinth of Gedref*

When Arthur killed a unicorn he unleashed a dreadful curse on Camelot. The only way the prince could undo his deed was to prove himself worthy and true of heart.

## Episode 12 – *To Kill the King*

Gwen's father, Tom, was seduced by a sinister sorcerer who claimed to have the power to turn lead into gold. When Tom was discovered by Uther's men the king ruthlessly sentenced him to death. Gwen was distraught and Morgana was determined to take her revenge: she was determined she would kill the king.

## Episode 13 – *Le Morte D'Arthur*

A Cockatrice had been hunting in the forest surrounding Camelot so Arthur and his party headed out to kill the beast. Although they managed to corner the creature, Arthur was bitten and Gaius delivered the terrible news that the bite of a Cockatrice is fatal. As Arthur's life hung in the balance, Merlin was the only one who could save him – but at what cost?

# Series 2

### Episode 1 – *The Curse of Cornelius Sigan*
When excavations beneath Camelot uncovered a tomb full of
gold and jewels, a petty thief unwittingly unleashed the spirit of
a powerful and ancient sorcerer, and Merlin had to risk his very
soul to save the kingdom from destruction.

### Episode 2 – *The Once and Future Queen*
Merlin helped Arthur disguise his identity to enter a jousting
tournament, little knowing that a deadly assassin had arrived in
Camelot to kill the prince. Forced to hide in Gwen's chambers
whilst the tournament was in progress the crown prince and the
maidservant started to fall in love . . .

### Episode 3 – *The Nightmare Begins*
When Morgana began to fear she might have magic, Merlin
put both their lives at risk to get her the help and guidance she
needed.

### Episode 4 – *Lancelot and Guinevere*
When Gwen was kidnapped Arthur defied the king to go to her
rescue, but someone else got there first: Lancelot.

### Episode 5 – *Beauty and the Beast – Part One*
Uther was delighted when the beautiful Lady Catrina arrived
in Camelot but Merlin was concerned. After some careful
investigation he discovered the Lady was not all that she seemed:
Lady Catrina was a troll and she had her sights on marrying
Uther and taking control of Camelot.

### Episode 6 – *Beauty and the Beast – Part Two*
Merlin had to reveal that Camelot's new Queen was a malicious
troll before she destroyed the kingdom and all its people.

### Episode 7 – *The Witchfinder*
Uther summoned Aredian the Witchfinder to Camelot to root
out magic once and for all. It was to take all of Merlin's cunning
and bravery to protect both himself and his closest friends from
being condemned to death.

### Episode 8 – *The Sins of the Father*
A mysterious warrior arrived in Camelot and challenged Arthur
to a duel. When he realised this knight was a woman called
Morgause Arthur was stunned! On leaving the city she revealed
she once knew Arthur's mother, intrigued, he agreed to follow
her and so embarked on a quest that would reveal information
about his past that would change his life forever.

### Episode 9 - *The Lady of the Lake*
On a dark night in Camelot, Merlin met a kindred spirit. But
his new friendship with the mysterious Freya was threatened
when a magical beast unleashed a series of deadly attacks in
the city.

### Episode 10 – *Sweet Dreams*
Camelot was thrown into chaos when a rival king placed a spell
on Arthur in an attempt to start war between the kingdoms.

### Episode 11 – *The Witch's Quickening*
Merlin witnessed a shocking side to Morgana when Mordred,
accompanied by a sinister sorcerer with robbery and murder on
his mind, arrived in Camelot asking for her help.

### Episode 12 – *The Fires of Idirsholas*
Furious at her failed attempts to ruin Uther, Morgause
summoned the Knights of Medhir. This band of seven wraiths,
formerly noble knights whose souls where corrupted by an evil
sorcerer, were lethal warriors. As Morgause and her inhuman
knights attacked a helpless Camelot, Merlin's loyalties were
stretched to the limit.

### Episode 13 – *The Last Dragonlord*
When the Great Dragon attacked Camelot, Merlin embarked
on an epic journey to find the last Dragonlord, the one man
who could defeat the monster. He did not expect this quest
would lead him straight to his father.

# INDEX

# MORE EXCITING MERLIN BOOKS!

THE MAGIC BEGINS

POTIONS AND POISON

SWORD AND SORCERY

A FIGHTING CHANCE

DANGEROUS QUESTS

MERLIN
The Dragon's Call

MERLIN
Valiant

MERLIN
The Mark of Nimueh

MERLIN
The Poisoned Chalice

MERLIN
The Death of Arthur

MERLIN
The Labyrinth of Gedref

QUEST ACTIVITY BOOK

FREE! PULL-OUT GAME

MYSTERY ACTIVITY BOOK

FREE! MAGIC NOTEBOOK

POTIONS & SPELLS ACTIVITY BOOK

100 FREE STICKERS

THE COMPLETE GUIDE